GOD CREATED the WORLD and the Universe

Written and Illustrated by
EARL and BONITA SNELLENBERGER

Copyright © 1989 by Eabon Design and Master Books
ISBN 0-89051-149-7   Printed in China

The Genesis account of Creation in our Bible has been translated from the Hebrew language into English. Knowing the meaning of the original Hebrew words can give us a deeper understanding of Scripture.

IN THE BEGINNING GOD CREATED THE HEAVENS AND THE EARTH (Genesis 1:1).

Time began when Eternal God created the heavens and the earth. *Shamayim*, the Hebrew word for "heaven (or heavens)" in Genesis 1:1, has the meaning of our modern term *space*. Just think, God even made the empty space in which He put the rest of His creations. God made earth, and *erets*, Hebrew for "earth," means the *matter* of the universe. Outer space was still totally dark. The unformed, empty earth and the formless waters God made were in darkness until He said, "Let there be light"—and there was light. Light is a form of *energy*.

Scripture mentions *three* "heavens." The spiritual *third* Heaven (Heb. 9:24; II Cor. 12:2-4) and the angels that dwell there (Dan. 7:10; Rev. 5:11; 9:16) were created at the *very* beginning of the first day. They did not exist before then, for Christ created everything (both visible and *invisible*) (Col. 1:16) within the six days of Creation (Exodus 20:11).

THE ANGELS REJOICED WHEN THE WORLD WAS CREATED.

Space, matter, and *energy* are the basis of the physical universe. And God made them *out of nothing!* How powerful and great God is. Little wonder that all of His angels shouted for joy to see Earth's creation (Job 38:4-7). God ended the first day of Creation Week by dividing the light from the darkness. The Sun had not yet been made, but God caused the light to shine upon the world and started the cycle of day and night. The Earth had been formed by the end of the first twenty-four-hour period, but was still not ready for life.

GOD FORMED THE EARTH INTO A SPHERE AND PREPARED IT FOR LIFE.

God "...set a compass upon the face of the depth (deep)" (Proverbs 8:27). "...He sitteth upon the circle of the earth" (Isaiah 40:22). On the second day, God separated "the waters above the *firmament*," meaning a stretched out space surrounding the world, from the waters below. On the third day, God gathered the waters under the firmament together to form seas and caused dry land to appear. Then God created grasses, herbs, and full-grown trees already bearing delicious fruit—each plant with seeds to reproduce its own kind.

The Sun, Moon, and stars are in the *second heaven* of outer space. (Isaiah 13:10).

GOD MADE THE LIGHTS OF THE HEAVENS ON THE FOURTH DAY: THE SUN TO RULE THE DAY, THE MOON TO RULE THE NIGHT, AND THE STARS.

On the first day of Creation, God had made rays of light that shone on the rotating Earth just as the Sun, Moon, and stars would do after He made them. Then on the fourth day of Creation, God said, "Let there be lights" (or 'light-givers') in the heavens (Genesis 1:14-19). God made our two great light-givers, the Sun and the Moon. After that the bright sun would shine upon the Earth to brighten the day and the pale moon would shine upon the Earth at night. He also made the stars and the planets. Isn't God's handiwork amazing?!

GOD CREATED SEA LIFE ON THE FIFTH DAY.

God said, "Let the waters bring forth abundantly the moving creatures that hath life...And God created great whales, and every living creature..." of the sea (Genesis 1:20,21). "Great whales" may include all very large sea creatures — even giant marine reptiles like plesiosaurs. Great whales may be referring to "great sea monsters" or "dragons." When God spoke, the waters suddenly swarmed "abundantly" with many, many different kinds of fish and other sea life.

Birds fly in the *first heaven* of Earth's atmosphere (Jeremiah 4:25).

GOD ALSO CREATED BIRDS ON THE FIFTH DAY.

When God made sea life, He also made "fowl that may fly above the earth..." (Genesis 1:20). Each "living creature" that God made was different from other creatures, yet each was perfect in its own way. God gave every creature exactly what it needed to live where He put it. God created fish with gills, scales, and fins to live in water. He gave flying birds lungs, light-weight bones, wings, and feathers to soar through the air. God blessed the sea life and birds, for He wanted each creature to reproduce young ones, after its own kind.

ON THE SIXTH DAY, GOD FIRST CREATED LAND ANIMALS.

"And God said, Let the earth bring forth the living creature..."—three groups of animals—"cattle, and creeping things, and beasts of the earth after his kind..." (Genesis 1:24). "Cattle" may represent what we would today call farm animals, animals which would live close to mankind and be useful to man in many ways. The term "creeping thing" could include insects and small animals such as turtles, frogs, snakes, and mice. "Beast of the earth" could include large wild animals such as elephants, rhinoceroses, and land dinosaurs.

THEN GOD MADE ADAM, THE FIRST MAN, IN HIS OWN IMAGE.

"And God said, Let *us* (Father, Son, and Holy Spirit) make man in *our* image, after *our* likeness..." God is three persons, yet He is one. For "...God created man in *His* own image..." (Genesis 1:26,27). Man is God's very special creation. Like the animals, man's body was made of the same elements as the earth. But unlike the animals, only "Adam was made a living soul..." (I Corinthians 15:45) and created in God's own image. God gave Adam rulership (dominion) over the animals and allowed Adam to name them (Genesis 2:19).

GOD CREATED EVE TO BE ADAM'S BRIDE.

God had made a male and female of each animal, but for Adam there was no mate. Then, in His last act of creation on the sixth day, God formed a woman from Adam's side (Genesis 2:20-24). God had created a perfect man and woman to live as husband and wife in the beautiful Garden of Eden. As God's steward, Adam was to care for the Garden. At that time, neither mankind nor animals ate meat—only plants. No animal killed and ate another at that time (Genesis 1:29,30). By God's command Adam and Eve were free to eat the fruit from any tree in the Garden, except one—the tree of the knowledge of good and evil.

"FOR IN SIX DAYS THE LORD MADE THE HEAVENS AND THE EARTH...AND ALL THAT IS IN THEM" (Exodus 20:11).

God pronounced everything that He had created to be *very* good. For at that time, all was perfect throughout the entire universe. In the *third* Heaven where God dwells, all the great hosts of angels God had created gave glory to Him. In the *second* heaven of outer space, the Sun, Moon, stars, and planets moved in perfect order. Above the firmament or *first* heaven, a blanket of water vapor may have surrounded the Earth, making the entire planet a tropical paradise. And God "rested on the seventh day"—not because He was tired (Isaiah 40:28-31), but as an example for man to work six days—then rest, and worship God on the seventh day.

THEN THE ANGEL LUCIFER REBELLED AGAINST GOD, AND THERE WAS WAR IN HEAVEN.

God created the angel Lucifer perfect in wisdom and beauty (Ezekiel 28:12-17). Lucifer was there when God created the Earth, but instead of continuing to glorify God, Lucifer wanted to rule the universe and be worshiped. So Lucifer led a great army of rebellious angels in an unsuccessful battle against God and His faithful angels (Rev. 12:7-9). Cast out of Heaven, Lucifer became Satan, or the Devil, the author of sin. On Earth, speaking through the serpent, the evil fallen angel led Adam and Eve into sin—first, by casting doubt on God's Word..."yea, hath God said?" and, finally, by convincing them to eat the forbidden fruit.

Before God drove Adam and Eve from the Garden of Eden, He clothed them in animal skins.

Thorns and thistles grew from the cursed ground, and life became very hard for Adam and Eve.

BY ADAM'S SIN CAME DEATH AND DECAY — THE PERFECT WORLD WAS CHANGED (Romans 5:12).

The moment Adam and Eve sinned and experienced spiritual death (separation from God), they also began to grow old and die physically. God's entire "creation was made subject to vanity" — that is, "The bondage of corruption" — and decay (Romans 8:19-22). The Earth began to "wax old, as doth a garment," and someday it "shall perish" (Hebrews 1:10-12). After Adam's fall, it became universally true that everything would eventually run down, grow old, wear out, die, decay, and return to the dust.

"FOR AS IN ADAM ALL DIE, EVEN SO IN CHRIST SHALL ALL BE MADE ALIVE" (I Corinthians 15:22).

God killed animals to clothe Adam and Eve to show them that "atonement" (or covering) for sin could only be provided by God through the shedding of innocent blood. And God gave Adam and Eve hope for fallen mankind through the promised coming of Jesus, the "Seed of the woman" (Genesis 3:15). Jesus' innocent blood was shed as the final sacrifice for sin—that those who turn to Him as Savior might have eternal life. Jesus "bruised the head" of "that old serpent called the Devil," and set us free from sin's bondage.

Violence filled the Earth

ADAM AND EVE HAD CHILDREN, AND THEIR CHILDREN MARRIED EACH OTHER AND HAD CHILDREN. MAN BEGAN "TO FILL THE EARTH."

In those days, men had many children because they lived to be hundreds of years old. Perhaps, in part, because the water vapor canopy that God placed "above the firmament" blocked out the aging effects of the Sun's powerful rays. Sadly, however, as man increased in numbers he became ever more sinful, until his thoughts were "only evil continually." And "the Earth was filled with violence." So God chose to destroy the world—all but a faithful man named Noah, his family, and the air-breathing land creatures that God sent aboard a huge ship, the Ark.

Every human being and air-breathing land creature outside the Ark died in the worldwide Flood of Noah's time.

The bones and shells of some creatures that were suddenly buried under tons of mud and water were turned into fossils.

ALL ON THE ARK WERE SAVED WHEN THE GREAT DELUGE DESTROYED THE WORLD OF NOAH'S TIME.

When Noah and his wife, their three sons and their wives, all of the animals, and a supply of food were aboard the Ark, God shut them safely in. Then the Great Deluge began. The vast water vapor canopy "above the firmament" collapsed to pour down upon the Earth for 40 days. And "all the fountains of the great deep (were) broken up" (Genesis 7:11), sending water gushing forth from the ground to bury billions of land animals, plants, and even sea creatures — layer upon layer — under tons of mud. Minerals in the mud and water turned some of them into fossils.

GOD CREATED the WO

THESE 32 STICKERS SHOW THE WORLD AND THE UNIVERSE IN THEIR NATURAL COLORS AS GOD MADE THEM. FIND THE MATCHING PICTURE FOR EACH STICKER.

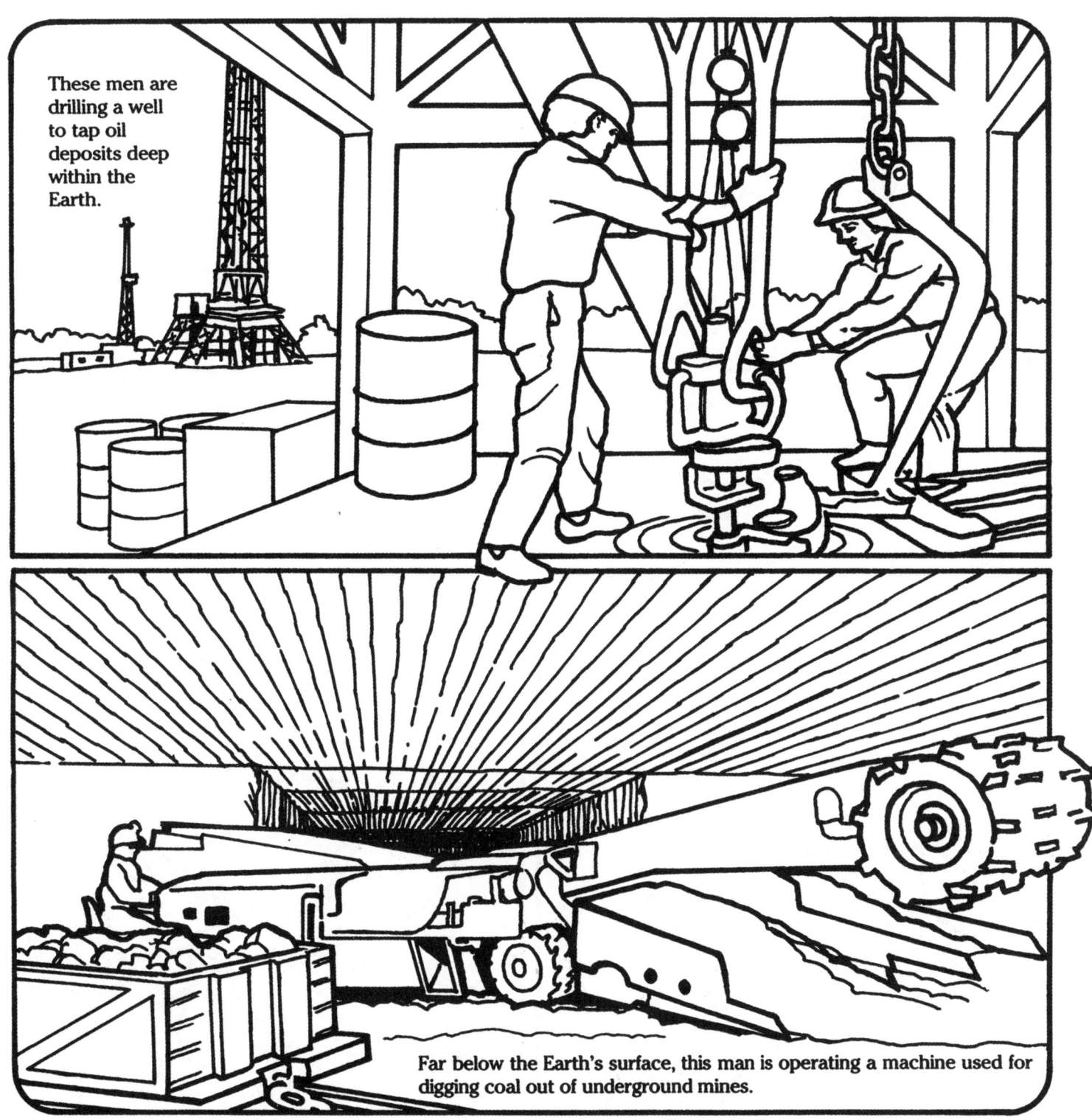

These men are drilling a well to tap oil deposits deep within the Earth.

Far below the Earth's surface, this man is operating a machine used for digging coal out of underground mines.

THE WORLDWIDE FLOOD NOT ONLY PRODUCED FOSSILS, IT ALSO PRODUCED SO-CALLED "FOSSIL FUELS"—OIL, GAS, AND COAL.

Untold billions upon billions of plants and living creatures were **rapidly** converted to coal, gas and oil by the tremendous pressure and heat from their burial under billions of tons of mud and water. In recent laboratory experiments, scientists have converted plant material into oil in only 20 minutes. Their use (and misuse) has also harmed mankind and the Earth— polluting the environment with acid rain and oil spills. God has given man dominion over the Earth, but as God's stewards our dominion requires responsibility. Man's dominion over the Earth is to provide for needs.

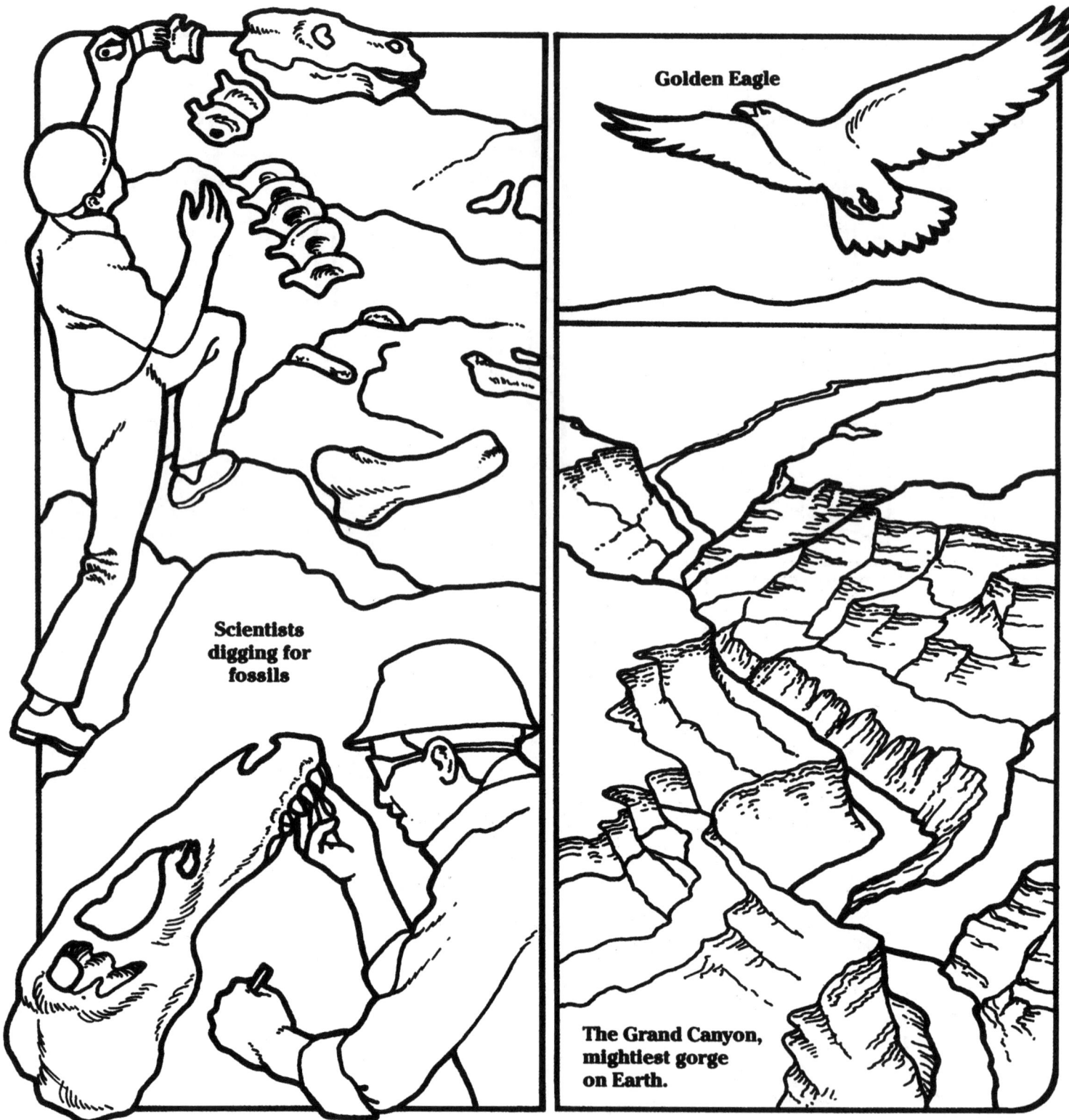

Golden Eagle

Scientists digging for fossils

The Grand Canyon, mightiest gorge on Earth.

FOSSILS, FOSSIL FUELS, AND THE GRAND CANYON ARE ALL VISIBLE SIGNS OF THE GREAT FLOOD.

To be completely covered by the Flood waters (Genesis 7:19-20), the mountains before the Flood must have been much lower than they are now. For God ended the Deluge by causing high mountains to rise up and deep valleys to sink down so that the Flood waters "fled" and "hasted away" into enlarged ocean basins (Psalms 104:5-9). Those rushing waters carved through layers of still soft Flood-deposited sediment. The Grand Canyon certainly came from this world-wide flood or waters left over from the Flood. Today, scientists carve through layers of hard sediment to find fossils—each one proof of the Great Flood.

Noah built an altar and shed the blood of innocent animals in sacrifice to God (Genesis 8:20-22) "And God blessed Noah and his (three) sons, and said . . . Be fruitful and multiply, and replenish the Earth" (Gen. 9:1).

AFTER 371 DAYS ON BOARD THE ARK, NOAH'S FAMILY CAME OUT INTO A CHANGED WORLD.

Perhaps plants growing in the Flood-eroded soil would no longer supply mankind proper nutrition—for God gave man permission to eat animals (Genesis 9:3). With the loss of Earth's water vapor canopy and warm oceans, snow and ice built up near the poles, and gigantic ice sheets spread out to cover large areas of newly formed continents. This Ice Age may have helped cause the extinction of dinosaurs and many other animals. In time, the Sun's warmth melted the icy glaciers and the Earth became as it is today. The Sun is part of God's plan to keep the Flood-changed Earth a life-supporting planet.

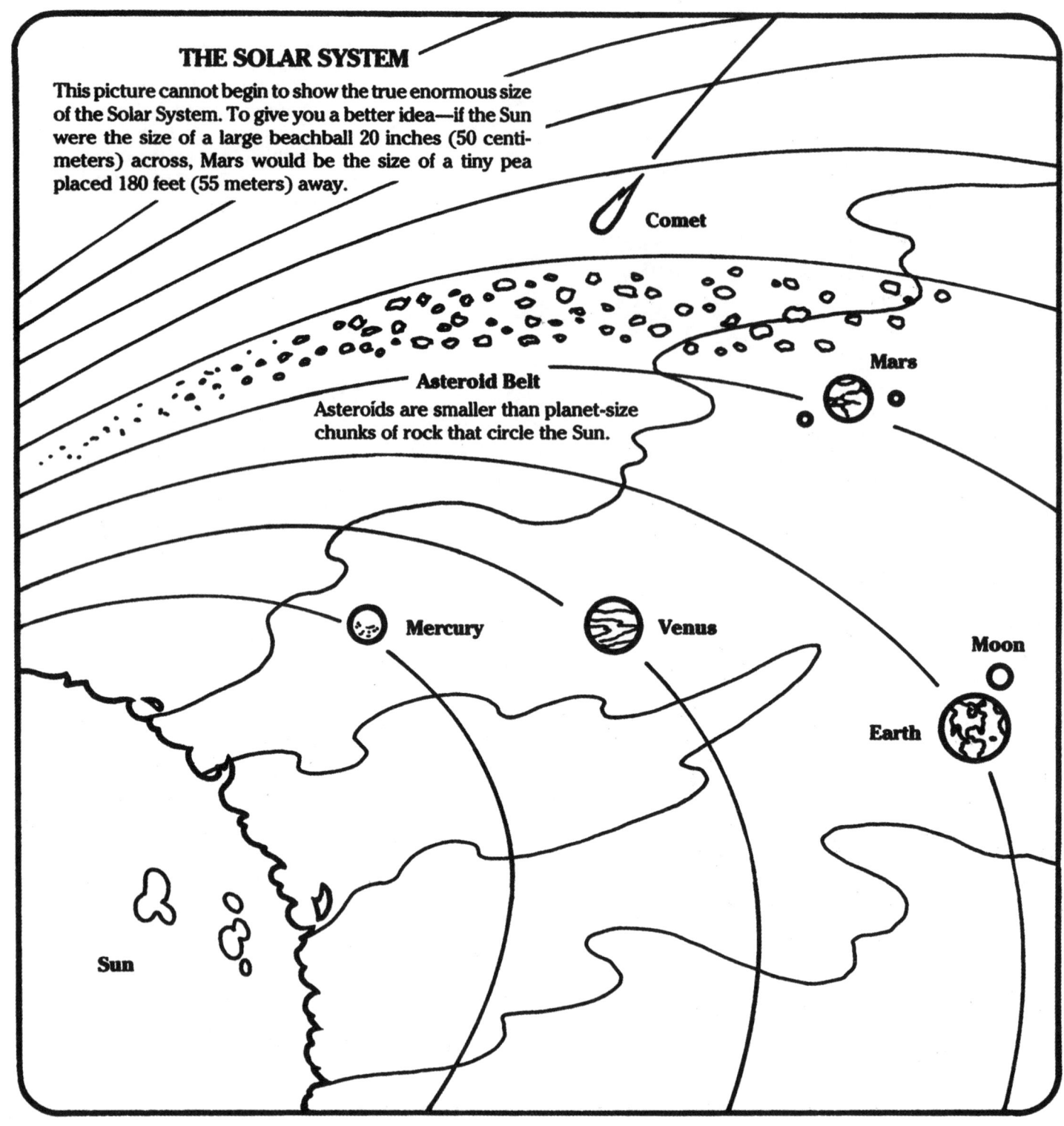

THE SOLAR SYSTEM

This picture cannot begin to show the true enormous size of the Solar System. To give you a better idea—if the Sun were the size of a large beachball 20 inches (50 centimeters) across, Mars would be the size of a tiny pea placed 180 feet (55 meters) away.

Asteroid Belt
Asteroids are smaller than planet-size chunks of rock that circle the Sun.

LIFE COULD NOT EXIST ON EARTH WITHOUT THE SUN. GOD PLACED THE SUN AT THE CENTER OF THE SOLAR SYSTEM WE LIVE IN.

The word '*solar*' means "of the sun." Our Solar System contains one star, our Sun. Nine planets, including Earth, orbit (circle in a path) around the Sun; and dozens of moons, in turn, orbit these planets. God created a force of attraction between all these heavenly objects called *gravity*. Gravity pulls a planet toward the Sun. But *inertia*—a planet's tendency to keep going straight—pulls the planet away from the Sun. God balances these two forces to hold each planet (and moon) in its perfect orbit.

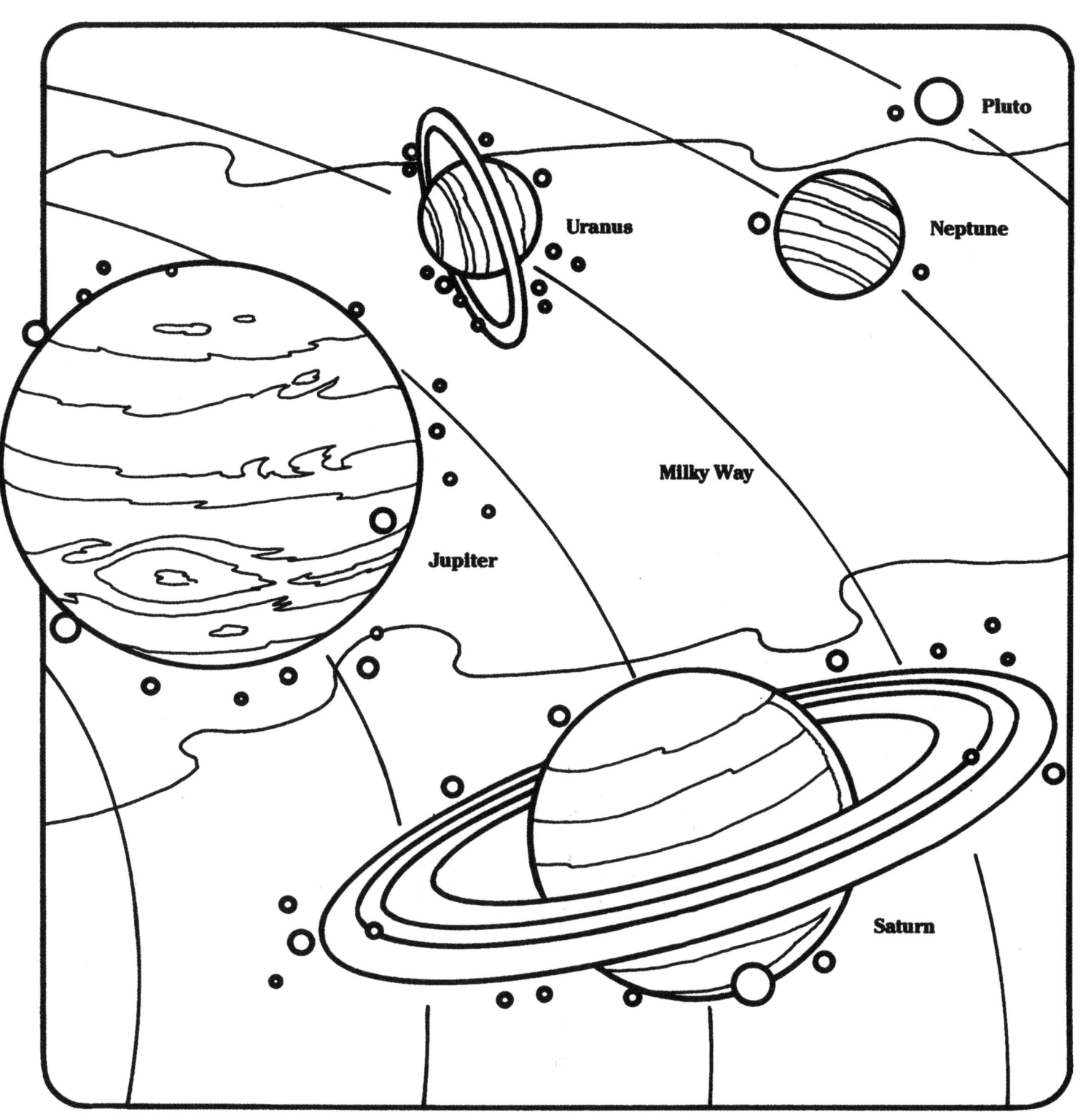

IT IS JESUS, THE WORD AND SON OF GOD, WHO UPHOLDS THE FORCE OF GRAVITY BY HIS POWER (Hebrews 1:3).

Gravity is a mystery! Modern science doesn't really know what causes its force. It *is* known, however, that *without* gravity, the Solar System would fly apart. But the same Jesus who created the Solar System sustains (upholds and supports) it. He established gravity and other natural laws. "...All things were created by Him (Jesus) and for Him...and by Him all things consist (or hold together)" (Colossians 1:16,17).

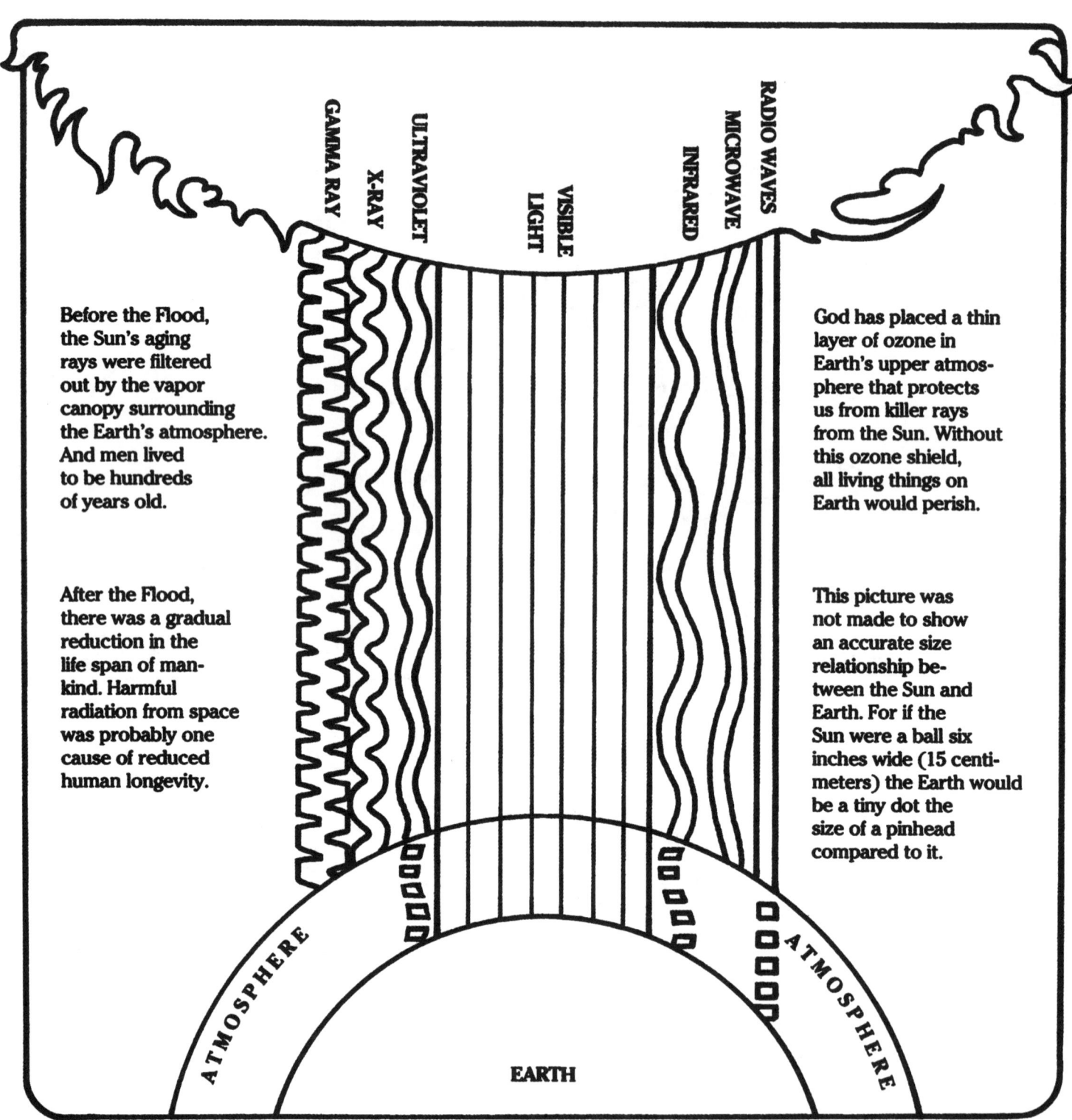

OUR SUN IS A STAR. AND LIKE ALL STARS, IT IS A GIGANTIC BALL OF HOT BURNING GASES.

God made the Sun to radiate powerful energy waves, some visible and some invisible. Only the wavelengths that make up the colors of the rainbow are visible to our eyes. But invisible ultraviolet waves tan our skin, and we feel infrared waves as heat. God has placed a protective envelope of air and a magnetic field around the Earth that filters and repels harmful energy waves from the Sun. The amount of energy the Earth receives from the Sun is just right to light our planet, keep us warm, and help plant and animal life grow.

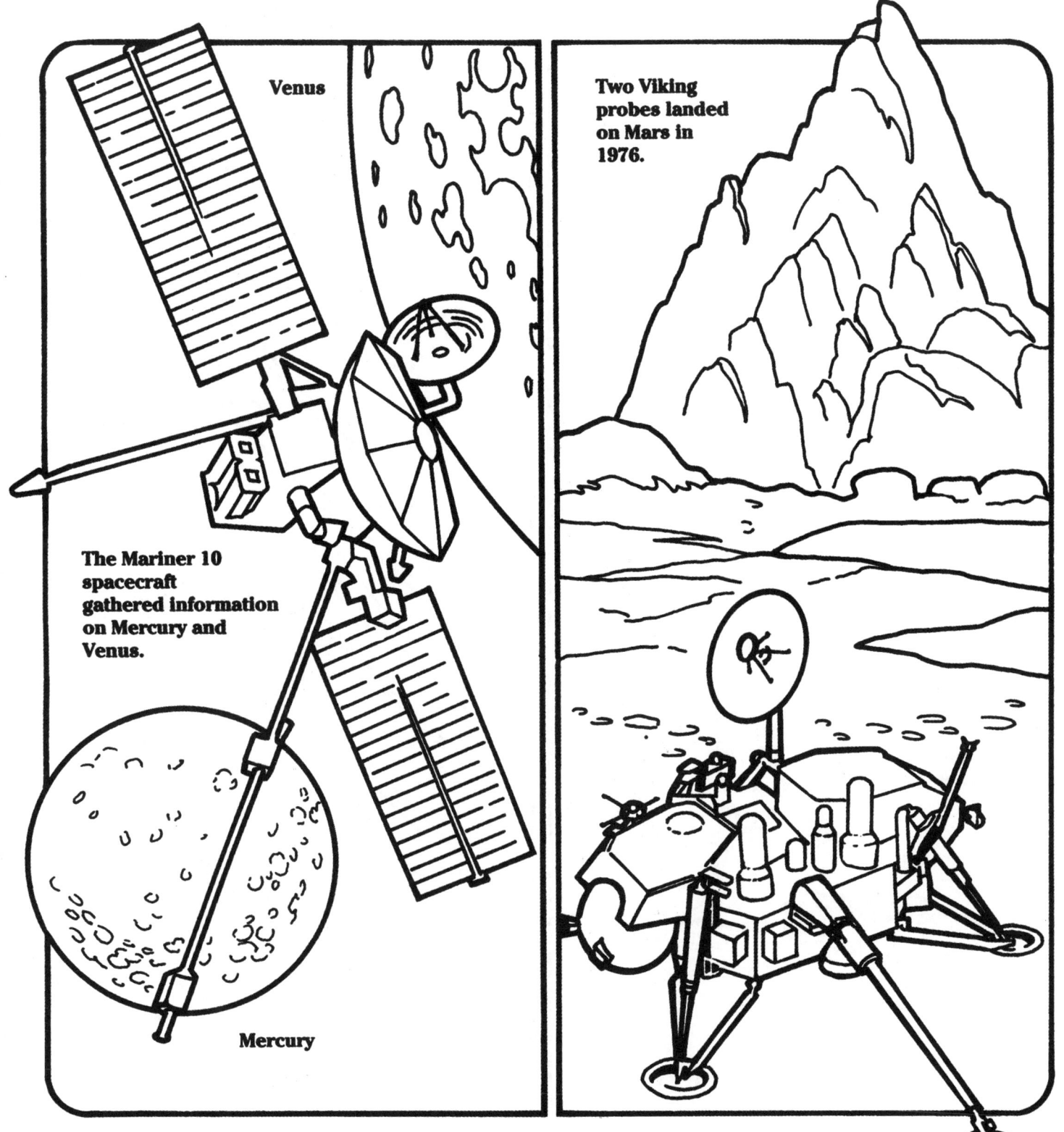

THE INNER PLANETS, THOSE CLOSEST TO THE SUN.

Information gathered by pilotless space probes have told us what it's like on our planet neighbors, Mercury, Venus and Mars. Airless Mercury, the planet nearest the Sun, is a ball of barren rock with a daytime temperature hot enough to melt lead. A blanket of carbon dioxide and poisonous sulfuric acid clouds makes the surface of Venus hotter than Mercury, although it is twice as far from the Sun. Mars, farther away from the Sun than Earth, is a cold world of dry, mountainous deserts. As Creation Scientists had predicted, there has been no trace of life whatsoever, found on any of these three, barren planets.

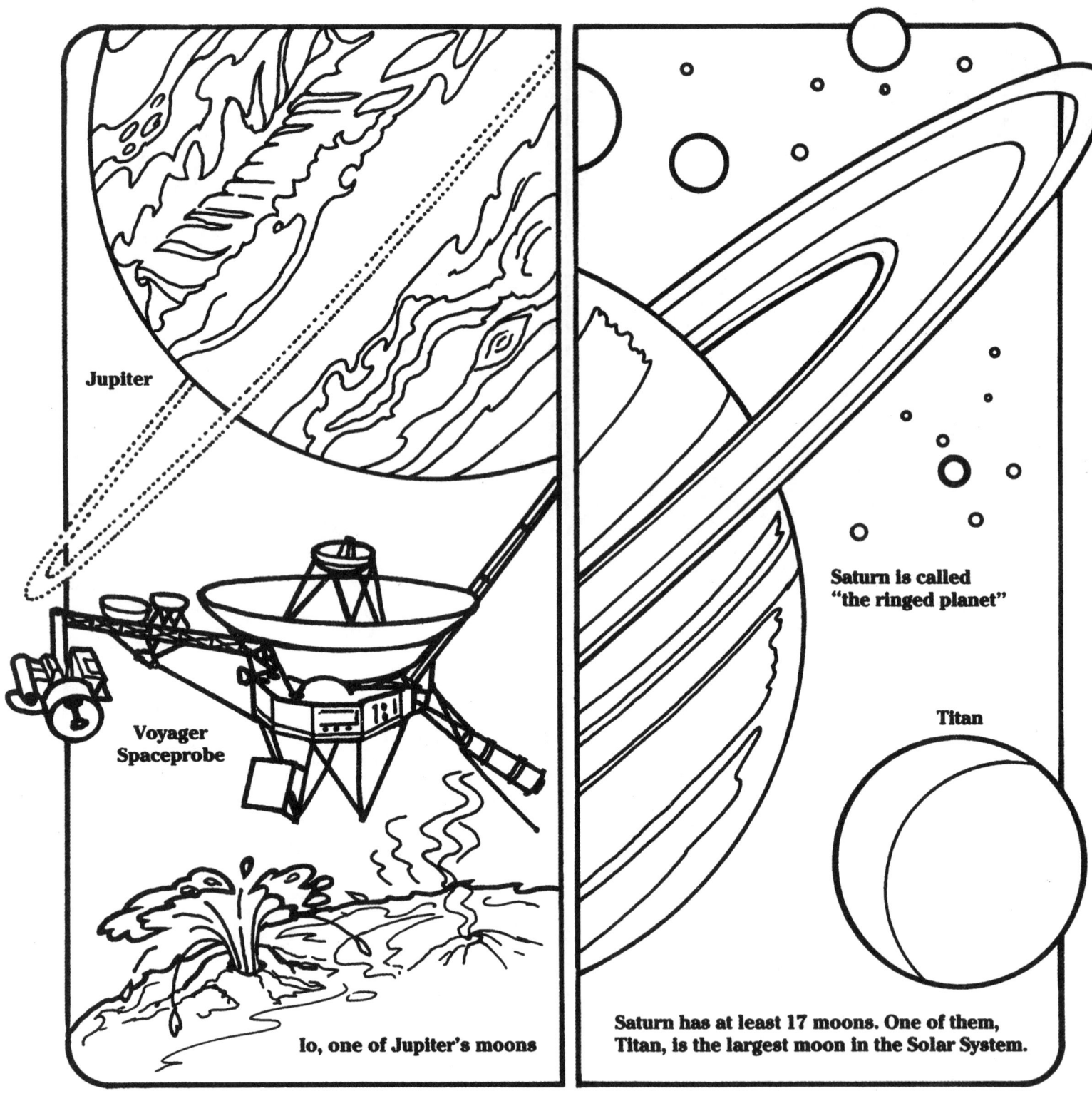

Jupiter

Voyager Spaceprobe

Io, one of Jupiter's moons

Saturn is called "the ringed planet"

Titan

Saturn has at least 17 moons. One of them, Titan, is the largest moon in the Solar System.

ARE THERE SIGNS OF LIFE ON THE OUTER PLANETS, FAR FROM THE SUN?

Unlike the four inner planets made of rock, Jupiter, the largest planet in the solar system, is a giant ball of gas that rages with violent windstorms. In 1979, the Voyager Spaceprobe's camera recorded a volcanic eruption on Io, one of Jupiter's many moons — another evidence that the Solar System is young! If it were very old, this small moon would have become cold and inactive long, long ago. Also, Voyager pictures showed that the beautiful rings of the huge gas planet Saturn are made up of ice and rock. And to no ones suprise, there was no life on Jupiter or Saturn!

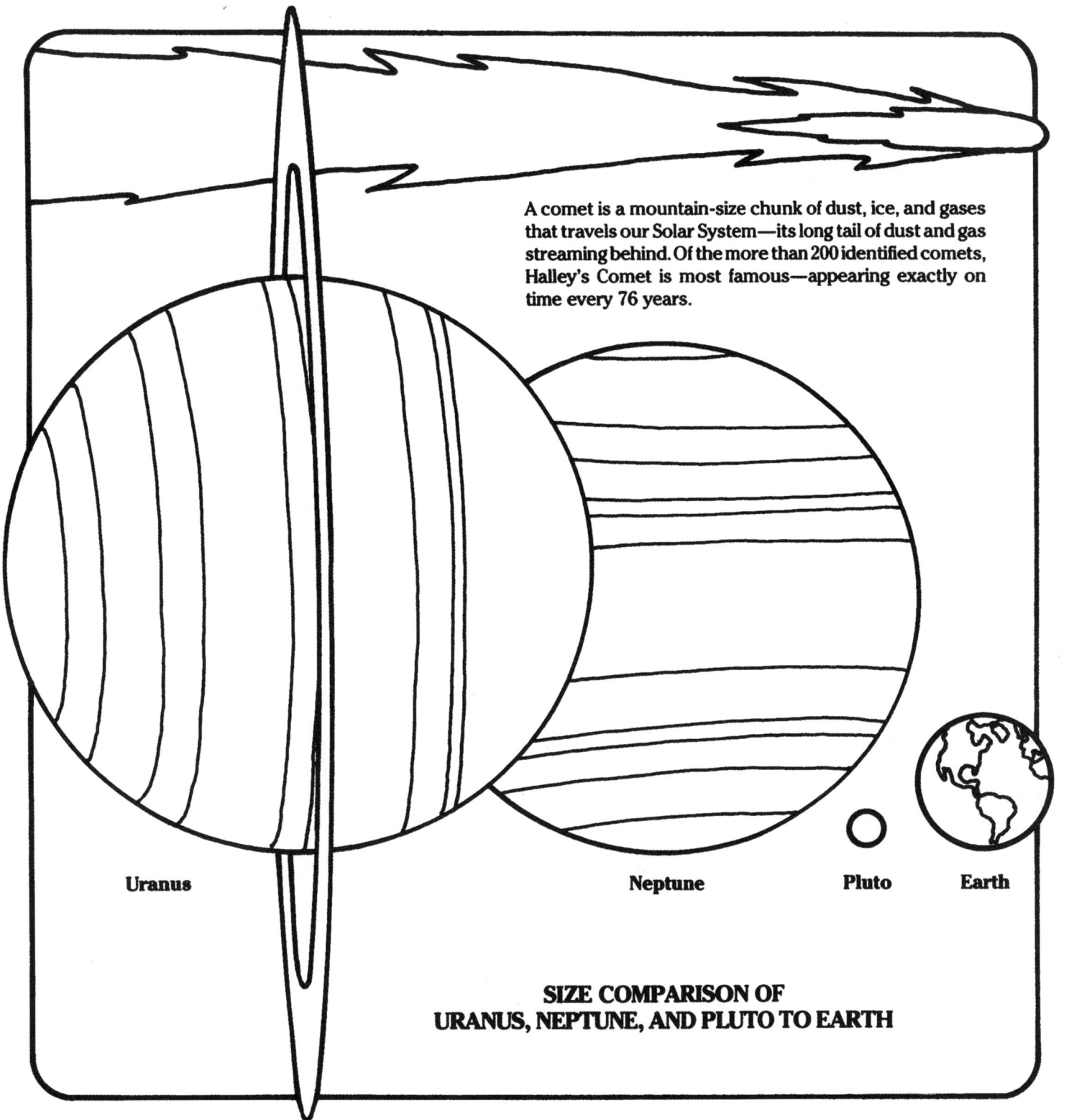

A comet is a mountain-size chunk of dust, ice, and gases that travels our Solar System—its long tail of dust and gas streaming behind. Of the more than 200 identified comets, Halley's Comet is most famous—appearing exactly on time every 76 years.

SIZE COMPARISON OF URANUS, NEPTUNE, AND PLUTO TO EARTH

URANUS AND NEPTUNE ARE GAS GIANTS. TINY PLUTO IS MOSTLY ROCK.

Uranus, closest of the three planets that lie out beyond Saturn, is 19 times further from the Sun than Earth. All other planets rotate horizontally, like a spinning top. But unusual Uranus rotates on its side, like a rolling ball! Uranus and Neptune appear greenish blue because of the poisonous methane gas clouds in their atmospheres. Distant Pluto, undiscovered until 1930, is the smallest planet in the Solar System. Far from the Sun, Uranus, Neptune and Pluto stay colder than -350 degrees below zero (-212 degrees Celsius). They are dead worlds. Life exists on one planet only — Earth!

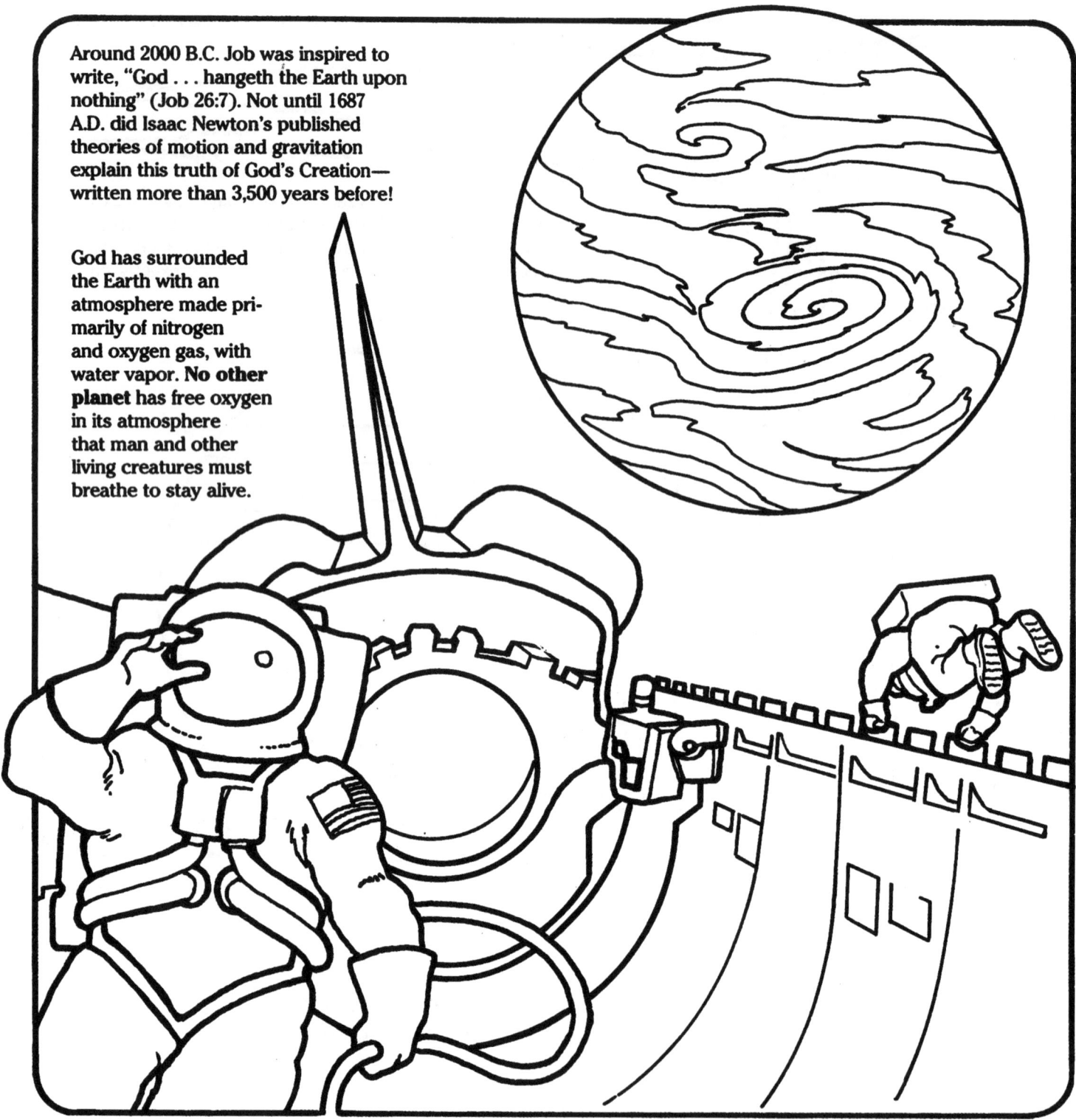

Around 2000 B.C. Job was inspired to write, "God . . . hangeth the Earth upon nothing" (Job 26:7). Not until 1687 A.D. did Isaac Newton's published theories of motion and gravitation explain this truth of God's Creation— written more than 3,500 years before!

God has surrounded the Earth with an atmosphere made primarily of nitrogen and oxygen gas, with water vapor. **No other planet** has free oxygen in its atmosphere that man and other living creatures must breathe to stay alive.

GOD HIMSELF FORMED THE EARTH . . . HE CREATED IT NOT IN VAIN, HE FORMED IT TO BE INHABITED (Isaiah 45:18).

Earth is the only planet where God put liquid surface water. "He founded (the Earth) upon the seas and established it upon the waters" (Psalms 24:2). Water, covering nearly three-fourths of Earth as liquid and suspended in air as vapor, makes life possible—and makes our world appear, from outer space, as a beautiful bright blue ball with swirls of white clouds. Life on Earth could not exist without water. It is necessary for all of life's key systems—respiration, circulation, digestion, and reproduction.

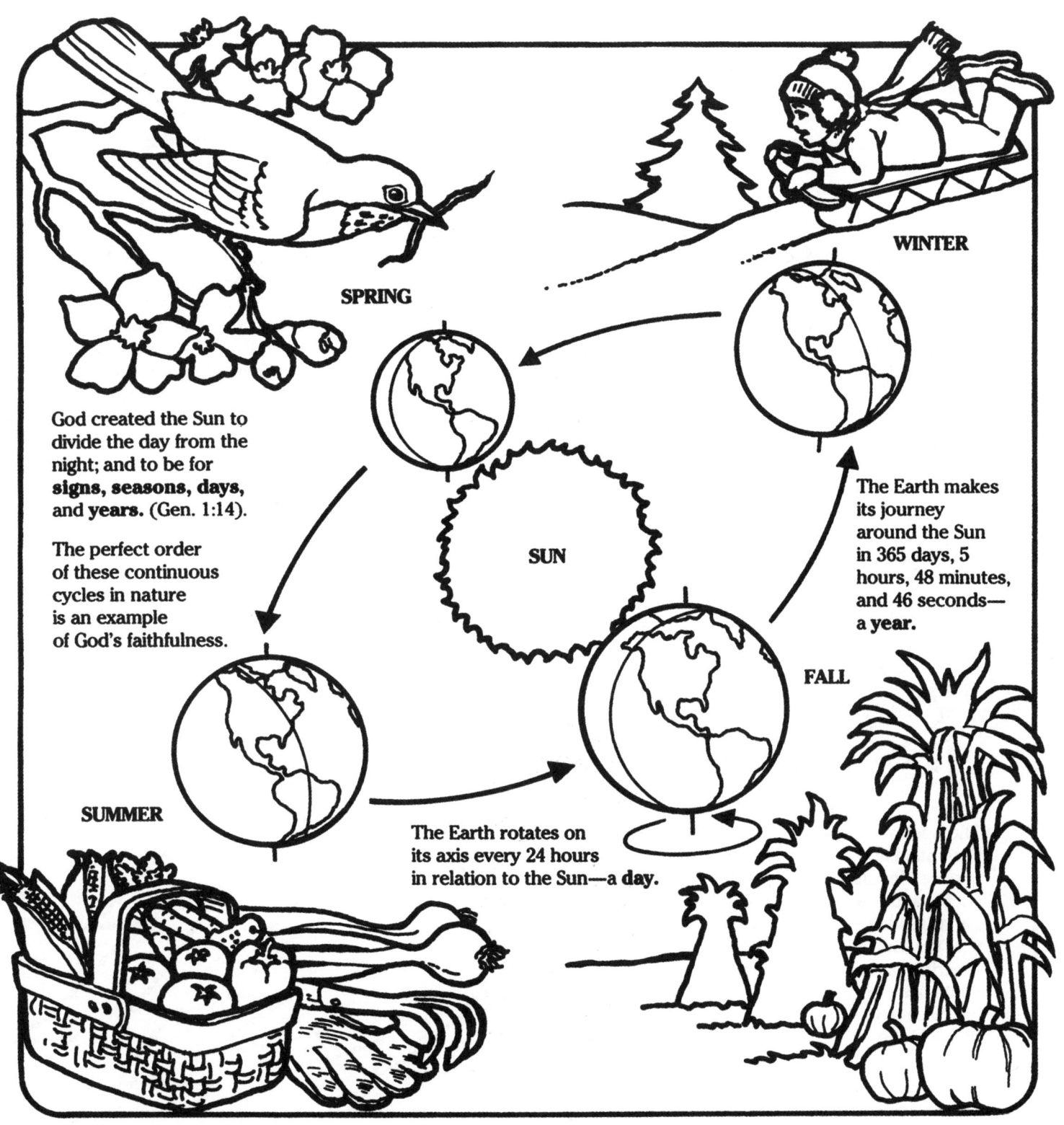

THE FOUR SEASONS, COLD AND HEAT, AND DAY AND NIGHT ARE CONTROLLED PRIMARILY BY THE EARTH'S RELATIONSHIP TO THE SUN.

Although the Great Flood caused great changes in the Earth, God promised Noah there would be a fixed, regular order of nature that mankind could depend upon (Genesis 8:22). God tilted the Earth's axis (an imaginary line going through Earth's center from pole to pole) at the perfect angle (23 degrees from the perpendicular) in relation to the plane of its orbit around the Sun to cause four seasons in the temperate zone. Cold and heat are balanced by Earth's perfect distance from the Sun. If Earth were closer, melting glaciers would flood many major cities.

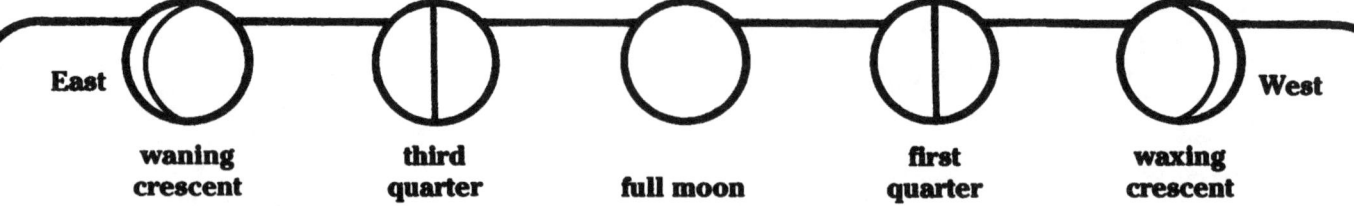

THE MOON'S PHASES

Unlike the Sun, the Moon does not **generate** light. As do Earth and the other planets, the Moon **reflects** light from the Sun. But like the Sun, God created the Moon to divide the day from the night; and to be for signs, seasons, days, and years. In fact, during Old and New Testament times, Israel's calendar was based on Moon phases—the changes in the Moon's appearance that take place during a month. From Earth, the Moon seems to gradually change shape. It grows from a thin, curved sliver, to a half circle, to a full circle, back to a sliver again, and then it seems to vanish altogether. This happens because we see different amounts of the Moon's sunlit side as it moves around the Earth. The Moon goes through its phases in 29½ days. In Israel, a new month began when the waxing crescent phase was first seen. And Hebrew festivals were scheduled around Moon phases (Numbers 10:10).

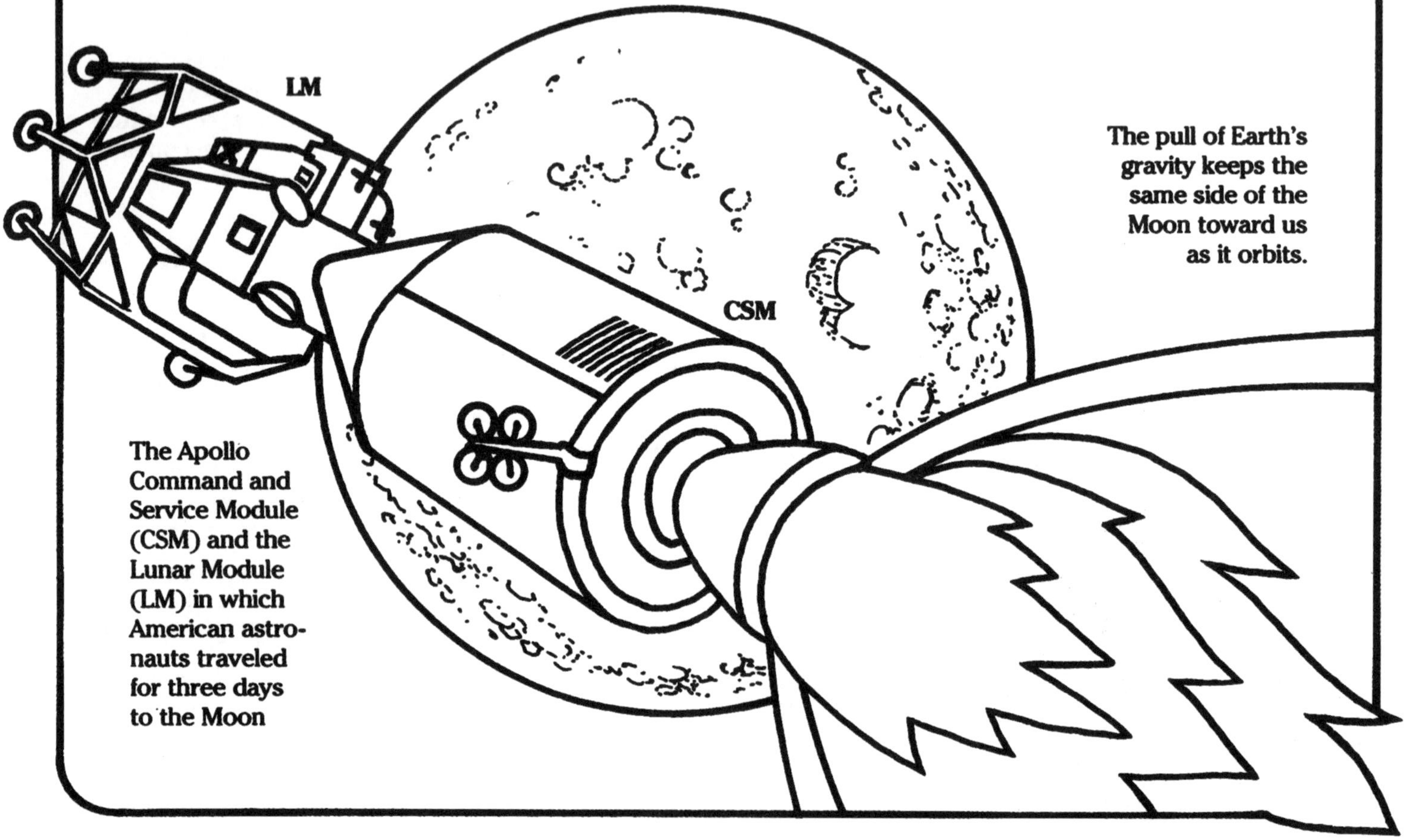

The Apollo Command and Service Module (CSM) and the Lunar Module (LM) in which American astronauts traveled for three days to the Moon

The pull of Earth's gravity keeps the same side of the Moon toward us as it orbits.

THE SURFACE OF THE MOON IS PITTED WITH CRATERS FROM BEING BOMBARDED BY METEORITES.

Men have viewed the Moon's craters with telescopes for over 300 years, but until the 1960's no one knew what the Moon's surface was **really** like. Tiny specks of cosmic dust continually rain down from outer space onto the Moon, Earth, and other planets. But the Moon, unlike the Earth, has no wind or water to sweep this dust away. Many scientists mistakenly believe the Moon is 4 1/2 billion years old—time enough for a very thick dust layer to gather. They were afraid that a landing spacecraft would sink into this dust and be unable to blast off for the return to Earth.

The Bible tells us the Moon was created suddenly (Psalms 33:6), from nothing (Hebrews 11:3).

ON JULY 20, 1969 THE MANNED APOLLO SPACECRAFT LANDED ON THE MOON.

Huge duck-feet landing pods were attached to the legs of the Apollo Lunar Module to help keep it from sinking into the expected deep, deep layer of cosmic dust. But astronaut Neil Armstrong stepped out onto just two to four inches (5 to 10 centimeters) of dust. The Moon appears to be quite "young"! It is also lifeless. And Moon rocks differ from rocks on Earth—proof that the Moon did not come from the Earth. The Moon is a special creation of God.

High Tide Low Tide

GOD MADE THE MOON SO ITS GRAVITATIONAL ACTION CAUSES THE EARTH'S TIDES.

As the Moon moves westward over the oceans, the water beneath it is pulled up to form a **high tide**, rising along waterfronts and covering beaches. As the Moon moves on, the water level drops to **low tide**, uncovering the beaches. Without the cleansing action of tidal water currents, the oceans along the Earth's seacoasts would stagnate — killing marine animals and plants. Isn't God wonderful! His tides always come on schedule, so ship captains can safely pilot and dock their vessels according to God's dependable tides.

David, the shepherd boy

Galileo was an astronomer, a scientist who studies the heavens.

"THE HEAVENS DECLARE THE GLORY OF GOD" (Psalm 19:1), WROTE DAVID WHEN HE LOOKED AT THE STAR-FILLED SKY.

David, the shepherd boy, could have counted over 3,000 stars with his unaided eye. Centuries later — over 300 years ago — an Italian astronomer named Galileo built one of the first telescopes. Looking through it Galileo was amazed when he saw thousands of new stars! But long before Galileo lived, God inspired Jeremiah to write that the starry "host of heaven" was too numerous to be counted by man (Jeremiah 33:22). Astronomers now estimate there are **ten million billion billion** stars in the known heavens — uncountable to man, but each star known to God by **name**! (Psalm 147:4).

A meteor, often called a "shooting star," is a small rock from space that passes through Earth's atmosphere and burns—making a streak of light.

The modern Hale Telescope on Palomar Mountain

DAVID ALSO WROTE, "O LORD...WHEN I CONSIDER THY HEAVENS...WHAT IS MAN, THAT THOU ART MINDFUL OF HIM?" (Psalm 8:3-4).

Our Solar System is part of the Milky Way, **a galaxy** of some 100 billion stars. And beyond the Milky Way are another 100 billion galaxies. In fact, modern telescopes and deep space probes find **no end** to God's Universe, yet the Universe has an end. The power of God is beyond our imaginations, yet God is still mindful of man. God so loved us He sent Jesus to Earth to be our Savior (John 3:16). For now, "creation groaneth...in pain" because of sin (Romans 8:22). So let us be good stewards "in this present world," looking for the glorious return to Earth of Jesus Christ who will make all things new.